Elvis Presley
25th Anniversary Songbook

ISBN 0-634-05274-8

HAL•LEONARD®
CORPORATION
7777 W. BLUEMOUND RD. P.O. BOX 13819 MILWAUKEE, WI 53213

Visit Hal Leonard Online at
www.halleonard.com

CONTENTS

ALL SHOOK UP

Words and Music by OTIS BLACKWELL
and ELVIS PRESLEY

A - well - a, bless my soul, __ what's wrong with me? __ I'm itch - ing like a man __ on a fuz - zy tree. __ My friends say I'm act - in' queer as a bug, __ I'm in love! __ I'm all shook up! __ Mm __

BLUE EYES CRYING IN THE RAIN

Words and Music by
FRED ROSE

ALMOST IN LOVE

Words by RANDY STARR
Music by LUIS BONFA

Moderately slow Rhumba

Your _____ lips were made for kiss - es so ten - der; ___

I'm al - most in love to - night.

ARE YOU LONESOME TONIGHT?

Words and Music by ROY TURK
and LOU HANDMAN

Moderately

Chorus

Are You Lone-some To-night, Do you miss me to-night, Are you

sor-ry we drift-ed a - part? _____ Does your mem-o-ry

stray To a bright sum-mer day, When I kissed you and called you sweet-

A BIG HUNK O' LOVE

Words and Music by AARON SCHROEDER
and SID WYCHE

BLUE SUEDE SHOES

Words and Music by
CARL LEE PERKINS

BURNING LOVE

Words and Music by
DENNIS LINDE

Lord a-might-y, I feel my tem-p'ra-ture ris - ing
Ooh hoo hoo, I feel my tem-p'ra-ture ris - ing.

CAN'T HELP FALLING IN LOVE

from the Paramount Picture BLUE HAWAII

Words and Music by GEORGE DAVID WEISS,
HUGO PERETTI and LUIGI CREATORE

CRYING IN THE CHAPEL

Words and Music by
ARTIE GLENN

DON'T

Words and Music by JERRY LEIBER
and MIKE STOLLER

DON'T BE CRUEL
(To a Heart That's True)

Words and Music by OTIS BLACKWELL
and ELVIS PRESLEY

Don't be cruel _____ to a heart that's true.
Don't be cruel _____ to a heart that's true. _
say. Don't be cruel _____ to a heart that's true. _

I don't

want no oth - er love. _____ Ba - by, it's just
Why should we be a - part, I real - ly, real - ly love you,

you I'm think - in' of. _____
ba - by, cross my heart. _____

(Now and Then There's)
A FOOL SUCH AS I

Words and Music by
BILL TRADER

Moderately slow, with expression

C6   C#dim7   G/D   E7   Am   Dm7

mf   *poco rit.*

G7   C   E7

Par - don me,   if I'm   sen - ti - men - tal,

a tempo

F   C   F/A   Ab7b5   C/G   Adim7   C/G

when we say good - bye.   Don't be an - gry with

Em7b5   A7   Dm   Dm7/A Dm7b5/Ab G7   C

N.C.

me,   should I   cry. _____   When you're gone,   yet I'll

FRANKIE AND JOHNNY

Words and Music by ALEX GOTTLIEB,
FRED KARGER and BEN WEISMAN

Medium blues

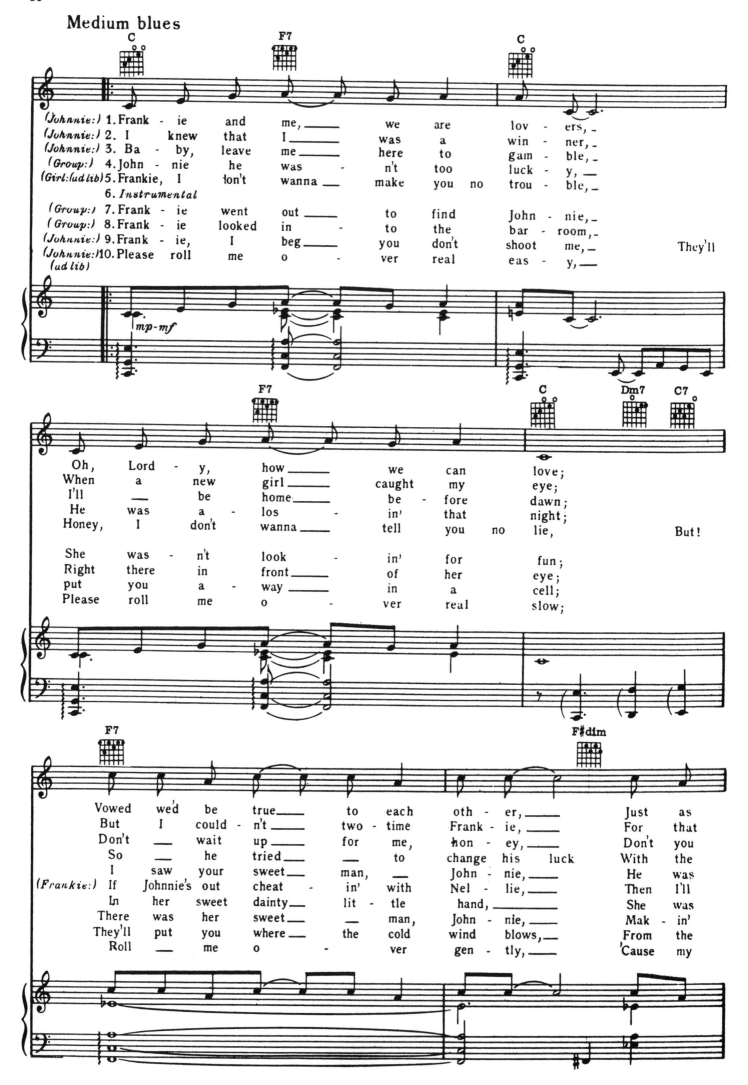

GOOD LUCK CHARM

Words and Music by AARON SCHROEDER
and WALLY GOLD

HEARTBREAK HOTEL

Words and Music by MAE BOREN AXTON,
TOMMY DURDEN and ELVIS PRESLEY

though it's al-ways crowd-ed, you still can find__some room for bro-ken-heart-ed lov-ers__ to

cry a-way__ their gloom.__ They'll be so, they'll be just so lone-ly, ba-by,

they'll be just so lone-ly, they'll be so lone-ly__ they could die. Now the

bell-hop's tears keep flow-ing; the desk clerk's__ dressed in black. Well, they've

Heart - break Ho - tel where you will be, will be just so lone - ly, ba - by,

well, you'll be lone - ly. You'll be so lone - ly ___ you could die.

A9

Piano solo ad lib.

HARD HEADED WOMAN

Words and Music by
CLAUDE DeMETRUIS

HIS LATEST FLAME

Words and Music by DOC POMUS
and MORT SHUMAN

HOUND DOG

Words and Music by JERRY LEIBER
and MIKE STOLLER

I WANT YOU, I NEED YOU, I LOVE YOU

Words by MAURICE MYSELS
Music by IRA KOSLOFF

I WILL BE TRUE

Words and Music by
IVORY JOE HUNTER

I _____ will _____ be true, no mat - ter

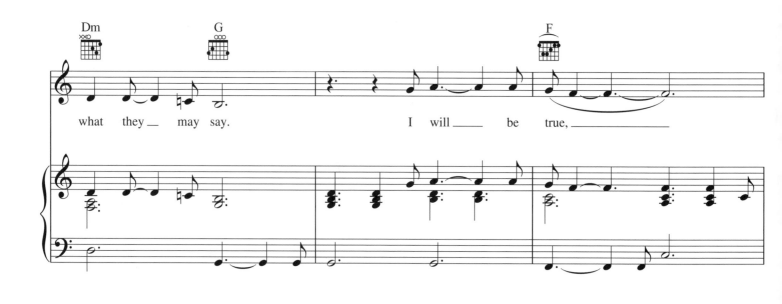

what they _ may say. I will _____ be true, _____

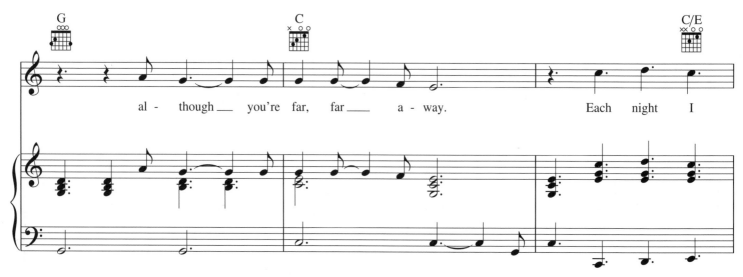

al - though _ you're far, far _____ a - way. Each night I

IN THE GHETTO
(The Vicious Circle)

Words and Music by
MAC DAVIS

To Coda ⊕

Then one night, in des-per-a-tion, the young man__ breaks a-way.__ He

I'M BEGINNING TO FORGET YOU
(Like You Forgot Me)

Words and Music by
WILLIE PHELPS

Moderately slow Blues

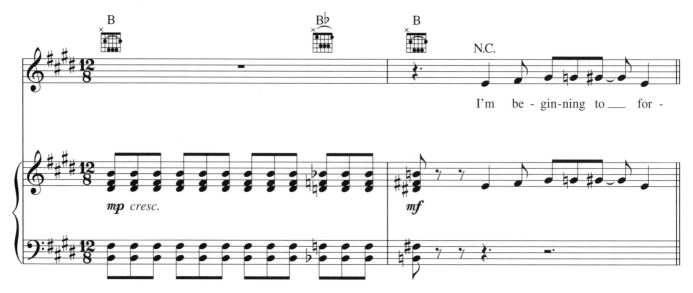

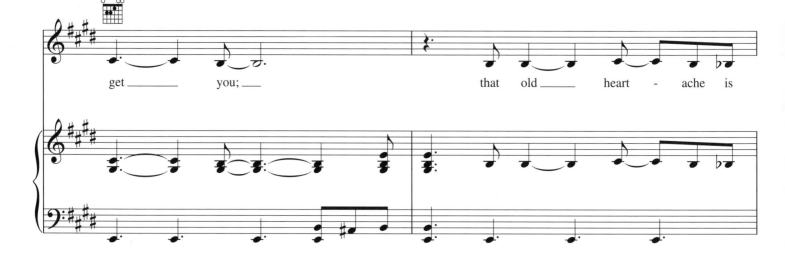

IT'S NOW OR NEVER

Words and Music by AARON SCHROEDER
and WALLY GOLD

JAILHOUSE ROCK

Words and Music by JERRY LEIBER
and MIKE STOLLER

Chorus

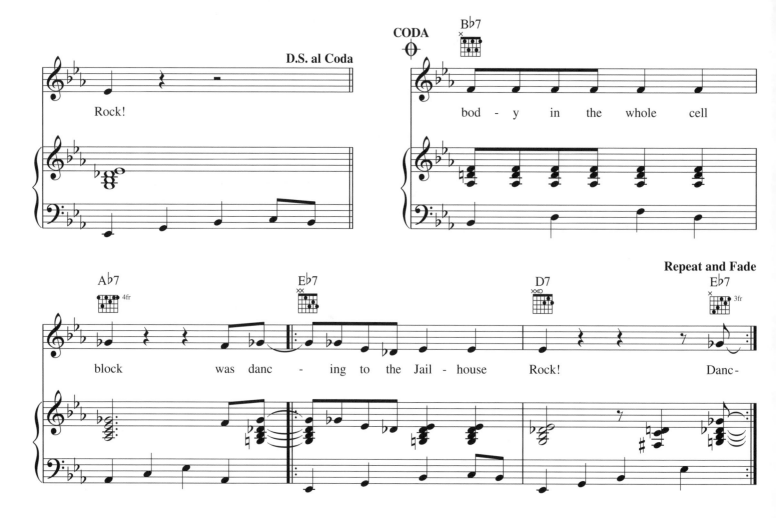

Additional Lyrics

2. Spider Murphy played the tenor saxophone
   Little Joe was blowin' on the slide trombone.
   The drummer boy from Illinois went crash, boon, bang;
   The whole rhythm section was the Purple Gang.
   (Chorus)

3. Number Forty-seven said to number Three:
   "You're the cutest jailbird I ever did see.
   I sure would be delighted with your company,
   Come on and do the Jailhouse Rock with me."
   (Chorus)

4. The sad sack was a-sittin' on a block of stone,
   Way over in the corner weeping all alone.
   The warden said: "Hey, Buddy, don't you be no square,
   If you can't find a partner, use a wooden chair!"
   (Chorus)

5. Shifty Henry said to Bugs: "For heaven's sake,
   No one's lookin', now's our chance to make a break."
   Bugsy turned to Shifty and he said: "Nix, nix;
   I wanna stick around a while and get my kicks."
   (Chorus)

KING CREOLE

Words and Music by JERRY LEIBER
and MIKE STOLLER

LITTLE SISTER

Words and Music by DOC POMUS
and MORT SHUMAN

ter.
tails.
ter,

Oh, I took her to____ the show.____
Hey, girl, I pinch your turned up nose.____
Lord, she's with some- bo - dy new.____

____ Hey, I went for some can - dy, a long____
____ Aw, but ba - by, you've been grow - in' and late la-
____ Aw, she's mean and she's e - vil like a

____ came it's Jim Dan - dy and they slipped right out____ the door.____
- ly been show - in' from head down to____ your toes.____
lit - tle old boll wee - vil, think I'll try my luck____ with you.____

THE MIRACLE OF THE ROSARY

Words and Music by
LEE DENSON

Original key: B major. This edition has been transposed up one half-step to be more playable.

LOVE ME TENDER

Words and Music by ELVIS PRESLEY
and VERA MATSON

RETURN TO SENDER

Words and Music by OTIS BLACKWELL
and WINFIELD SCOTT

STUCK ON YOU

Words and Music by AARON SCHROEDER
and J. LESLIE McFARLAND

You can shake an ap-ple off an ap-ple tree.__
Gon-na run my fin-gers thru your long black hair.__

Shake-a shake-a, sug-ar, but you'll nev-er shake me.__ Uh-uh - uh.__
Squeeze_ you _tight-er than a griz-zly bear.. Uh-huh-huh.__

No-sir - ee,__ uh-uh.__ I'm gon - na
Yes-sir - ee,__ uh-huh.__ I'm gon - na

SHE'S NOT YOU

Words and Music by DOC POMUS,
JERRY LEIBER and MIKE STOLLER

SURRENDER

Original Italian Lyrics by G.B. DE CURTIS
English Words and Adaptation by DOC POMUS
and MORT SHUMAN
Music by E. DE CURTIS

SWEET ANGELINE

Words and Music by CHRISTIAN ARNOLD,
DAVID MARTIN and GEOFFREY MORROW

SUSPICIOUS MINDS

Words and Music by
FRANCIS ZAMBON

THAT'S ALL RIGHT

Words and Music by
ARTHUR CRUDUP

3. I'm leavin' town tomorrow, leavin' town for sure,

Then you won't be bothered with me hangin' 'round your door,

But that's all right, that's all right.

That's all right, mama, any way you do.

I oughta mind my papa, guess I'm not too smart.

If I was I'd leave you, go before you break my heart,

But that's all right, that's all right.

That's all right, mama, any way you do.

THINKING ABOUT YOU

Words and Music by
TIMOTHY BATY

I woke up ___ this morn - ing, and I tried ___ to call ___ you, ___
I de - cid - ed to try ___ just ___ one ___ more ___ time ___

but you weren't there, ___ kind - a put me
to let you know ___ I real - ly

* *Omit whole notes when measure is repeated.*

TOO MUCH

Words and Music by LEE ROSENBERG
and BERNIE WEINMAN

TRUE LOVE TRAVELS ON A GRAVEL ROAD

Words and Music by A.L. "DOODLE" OWENS
and DALLAS FRAZIER

Down through the years, __ we've had hard times and tears, __ but they on - ly helped our love

grow, and we'll stay to - geth - er no mat - ter how strong the _ wind _ blows.

Not once have I seen your blue eyes __ fill with en - vy or

VIVA LAS VEGAS

Words and Music by DOC POMUS
and MORT SHUMAN

(Let Me Be Your)
TEDDY BEAR

Words and Music by KAL MANN
and BERNIE LOWE

Medium bright Rock

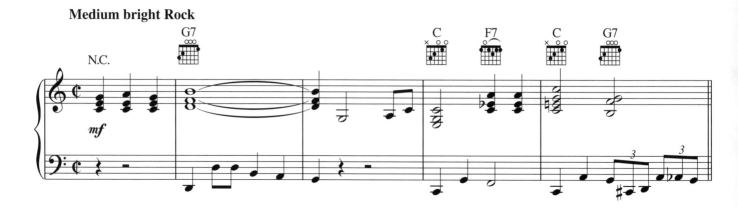

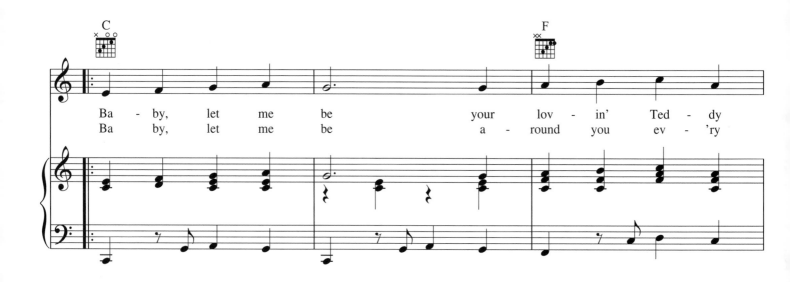

Ba - by, let me be   your lov - in' Ted - dy
Ba - by, let me be   a - round you ev - 'ry

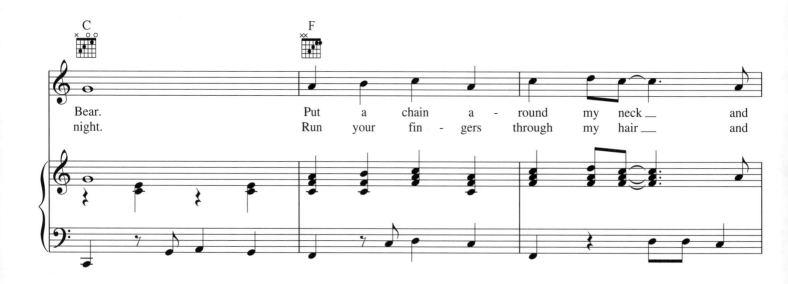

Bear.   Put a chain a - round my neck __ and
night.   Run your fin - gers through my hair __ and